SEASONS OF AFRICA

INSPIRING HOPE FOR CHANGE

SEASONS OF AFRICA

© 2011 by Nicholas Sibanda

Published by
Nicholson Integrated Consulting
P.O. Box 96295, Brixton 2092
Johannesburg
South Africa

www.nicholsonic.co.za

ISBN 978-0-620-51673-0

All rights reserved. No part of this book may be reproduced without written permission, except for brief quotations in books and critical reviews. For more information write to Nicholson Integrated Consulting or email niqsibanda@yahoo.com.

Unless otherwise noted, Scripture quotations are taken from the Holy Bible: The King James Version, Electronic Database.

Copyright © 1988-2006, by Biblesoft, Inc.

All rights reserved.

Contents

Dedication..5

Acknowledgements 6

Preface 7

Introduction...8

1. Our Rich Heritage 10

2. What is Wrong with Africa?...................................15

3. False Perceptions.. 21

3. Modern Africa..34

5. Governance Issues...40

6. Reorganising the People..56

7. Africa's Challenges..60

8. Where are we Headed...74

9. As a Nation Thinks.. 83

10. Bringing Change 90

Postscript...98

Dedication

To my children Minenhle Lerato, Luyanda Bokang, Jonathan Unathi and the millions of young people of Africa upon whom the future of our beautiful motherland is predicated. May they continue to represent the ideals that our fathers fought so hard to preserve for the generations to come.

Acknowledgements

Anyone who attempts to write a book knows the value of the important contributions of others in opening your eyes to the realities that shape you and your society. This is my first published book and in many ways informed by others.

My views were strongly shaped by my interface with students in universities as a staff in an IFES movement. I am grateful for the opportunity to see and believe in such great potential. I am grateful to many authors and speakers who instilled a fiery zeal for Africa in my heart. Some of them are quoted here and others are not.

Dr Myles Munroe's advocacy for Purpose helped me aspire for greater things for my people and myself. Dr Mensa Otabil shaped my biblical understanding of Black people. The Rev Dr David Zac Niringiye inspired me to put my ideas in writing. Dr Nevers Mumba, former Vice President of Zambia, is a true champion of African greatness.

I am grateful for the optimism of Rev. Lukhele of Zombodze Assemblies of God in Swaziland, who believes in the future of the continent shaped by young people. I am also indebted to the masses of ordinary, yet great Africans whose feelings and opinions I have attempted to represent in this book.

Preface

For Africa's sake

I have posted watchmen on your walls O Africa;
They will never be silent day or night
You who call on the Lord give yourselves no rest
And give him no rest till he establishes Africa
And makes her the praise of the earth.
Let the children of Africa arise
In the institutions of learning
Let them proclaim a new dawn of hope
And sing of the Lord's restoration.
From the Cape to Cairo
Senegal to Somalia
Let a new song of hope begin.
Home and away
They shall echo it aloud.
Count me in; May they say.
I stand in hope, I proclaim by faith
Let the tide swell
And sweep across this great continent.
Nkosi sikelel' iAfrica (God Bless Africa)

- © Nicholas Sibanda 2003

Introduction

The story of Africa is sometimes equally sad, as it is inspirational. The attempt by an individual to present her case to the world is, indeed, an ambitious task. As one of Africa's children though, I feel obliged to tell that part of the story that is personalised.

For Africa has for too long had her legacy retold by those not authorised and occasionally even by visitors! The intent of this book is to portray the story of the land in the experience of its own people. I t is the ideal future of the people and their rich inheritance that I seek to highlight. The core of its message is to interconnect the rich heritage with the current abilities to influence the outcome of the future.

I do not presume that this is an easy task. Yet it is important for the generation that shall implement change to be adequately informed and prepared. This book presents the story of Africa in time frames: Past, Present and Future. In each phase, it seeks to highlight the components that have always been overlooked by those who have told our story.

This has created serious misconceptions about Africa in the minds of those who are outsiders. However, there is an even greater tragedy when these opinions create a pessimistic outlook in the minds of the African people. It is a truth that no amount of pity or aid can emancipate a hopeless people. This book seeks to say to the African people; "There is hope in Africa for Africa." It is only when we put our trust in God and believe that He created us for a purpose that we will begin to see the change that our people so badly need. God made Africa and her time and season is due. It is time we as a people began to unleash the potential within us. We will start by looking back for inspiration and then forward for action.

Part 1

THE HISTORY AND HERITAGE OF AFRICA

One

OUR RICH HERITAGE

From the beginning of time, mankind has kept detailed record of their progress and significant experiences. The formats vary from ancient mythology, monuments, oral tradition, paintings, music and books to the litany of electronic gadgets used today. This fascination with history has helped man to find meaning in life and a basis for an effective interaction with his environment. History is a very real phenomenon. It is the foundation upon which individuals and communities define their existence. Our pursuits and accomplishments today are tomorrow's history, but no less important to our lives than they are today.

Actually, experiences tend to become more meaningful in retrospect. An African sage once said, "Life is lived forwards, but understood backwards." Because time is not static, the bulk of our communal existence consists of history, a manageable size of the present and a fair size lies in the future. Ignorance of the past therefore implies a severe limitation in living today and planning for the future. Similarly, a distorted vision of our historic background will inevitably lead to ineffective existence.

The histories of nations, families and individuals bear record and evidence that is essential to consider if they will gain a proper perspective to life. The chronological stages: past, present and future must be aligned if we shall be able to live our lives profitably. Some people opt for the selective approach where they only consider the good or the bad elements to define either themselves or others.

However, history presents us with a mixed bag and we do well to consider all its contents. For thus is human life defined. It is in celebrating the achievements and learning from the failures. We cannot 'simply ignore' some things and still retain a true picture of our identity. Our historic background is valid evidence for the case of life. Our future emerges from our past.

Africa's History

Biblical records and other historic writings from ancient tablets and very early scrolls ascribe a great deal to Africa. Civilisations, industry, technology, commerce, agriculture, politics and art emerged out of Africa in the ancient world.

Africa is the cradle of world turning civilisations. During famine periods, all roads led to Egypt where the grain never failed. The Egyptians had built top of the range irrigation facilities from the Nile. The revenue from international trade helped them build cities and develop a great deal of technology and arsenal.

Egypt manufactured all terrain, high speed chariots for war and travel and exported these and horses to the entire world. Advancement was happening on all fronts. The invention of the first writing pad in the form of papyrus took communication and literature to great heights. Structural engineering reached its peak when the pyramids were constructed. A great deal followed that history books account for in detail.

To the south, the Ethiopian kingdom emerged as one of the greatest exporters of African merchandise such as spices, gold and other precious stones. This kingdom was to be one of the chief contributors to the civilisation that we know of today. It was also a big player in the globalisation of Christianity.

These two African kingdoms contributed immensely to the world and were contributors to the development of the rest of the Near East and later Europe. The Age of Reason had a fair share of African greats such as St. Augustine of Hippo, Tertullian, Clement of Alexandria and many other philosophers of antiquity. These men influenced the development of growth of Christian thought and reason. They were later aptly recognised as the church fathers. The Western Kingdoms had their fair share of contribution in education and commerce. Further southwards, and over unrecorded years, oral history tells of exploits and heroes. Artefacts and rock paintings depict the genius of jungle survival with simple tools.

The evolution of lifestyles saw the invention of new technology for mining, agriculture and industry. Inter-tribal trade saw and emergence of alliances and later kingdoms. In the jungle existed medical specialists who could successfully developed cures for deadly diseases and epidemics.

On the political front, language experts, strategists and mediators brokered treaties and deals that made life better for all. Flourishing kingdoms, organised societies and rich cultures were established. Amazing art and structural genius such as the Great Zimbabwe stone city and many others are living evidence of the capability of the people across the ages. Icons and brave warriors such as King Shaka of the Zulu and others are founding fathers of our continental identity in later times.

In the modern world, facing new challenges and realities, Africa has not trailed behind. From the 1950's until 1990s she was breaking free from colonial rule. When the last of the shackles of apartheid were broken in South Africa, in 1994, it was one united effort and a sigh of relief. The new champions of this era include *among many*; Kwame Nkrumah of Ghana, Julius Nyerere of Tanzania, Robert Mugabe and Joshua Nkomo of Zimbabwe, Kenneth Kaunda of Zambia, Jomo Kenyatta of Kenya Samora Machel of Mozambique and Nelson Mandela of South Africa.

It should be stressed that there are many millions of others whose names are not listed but who contributed their life and soul for the liberation of our continent. They include villagers, women, schoolteachers, workers and young people. These made selfless sacrifices for our freedom. This Freedom is our special heritage and we must guard it jealously. It is freedom to be African and dignified members of the universal human family with full rights and responsibilities.

The darker side

However, despite the beautiful accomplishments, as with all other peoples, there is a darker side to the continent. Firstly, there were those who sold their own people to slave traders for personal gain and grossly abused their power and positions of authority. This was a sad betrayal of the heart and soul of Africa and her destiny. Not worse than that of other continents, yet still dark.

SEASONS OF AFRICA

In recent times, Africa has continually been plagued by the so-called civil wars that have reversed the gains of our bitter struggle against oppression. Clearly, greed, self-interest and power hunger are the factors behind it all. Indeed, there has always been a hidden foreign hand in it as well, but it found willing instruments amongst us.

We have seen rulers cling tenaciously to power even though their mandate was over, tearing apart the very fibre of their nations. Politicians who sought to consolidate their positions by dividing the people on tribal basis. It has happened all over the motherland in Rwanda, Nigeria, Zimbabwe, South Africa and Kenya to mention but a few examples. Laying aside the aspirations of unity, they pursue a contrived hollow ethnocentric agenda. They turn friends, neighbours and fellow countrymen one against the other.

In a bizarre climax of this orgy of hate, a million people were massacred in Rwanda in 1994. They were hacked to death with machetes and axes by their own people. That is a true shame for Africa because all that time the rest of us played dead and never said a word. Unfortunately, the streak of rivalry has stuck with us for much longer, growing and feeding on us like a wicked parasite that could finally destroy us. It is time we decided to put an end to this dark aspect that has so shamefully become a part of us.

Two

WHAT IS WRONG WITH AFRICA?

It is common to hear this question being asked in many quarters all through Africa. Many people have proposed likely answers to these questions. Some of these we shall discuss later as they tend to affect our self-perspective. Africa's history is inextricably defined by the events and actions imposed on her by others. The after-effects of colonial brainwashing are still rampantly evident in our offspring. Abolished in writing but alive and well in our conversation and lifestyles. So sadly, do we groom each generation to aspire to be "white" and *unAfrican*. Although this is induced, the responsibility to change it is ours. Untold numbers of Africans believe that we are an inferior race.

In truth, there actually *is* something wrong with Africa. How could a continent so richly endowed with cultural and natural resources such as diamonds, gold, wildlife, oil and vast acreage of fertile soil be ranked the poorest in the world? How could the people who fought for our freedom soon turn and be the oppressors themselves? Why would people who rose from the ashes soon forget those who made sacrifices to lift them up? Why are so many progressive Africans rich and famous yet their villages and towns are still backward and forgotten in the past? How do we end up with the bulk of the world's HIV/AIDS infection and death statistics?

Africa's greatest problems have to do with her identity. Most of us have never discovered the dignity of being African. The very term "African" has a derogatory connotation in certain parts of the continent. It implies inferiority, ugliness, ignorance and irrationality. When put with other races we tend to shrink back and want to apologise for our existence!

This concept of inadequacy is introduced to an African mind at a very early stage. Mostly, unconsciously. The generations before us were taught and learnt through experience that Africans were the lowest class of human beings. We have heard of the distorted creation story as quoted by Mensa Otabil in *Beyond the Rivers of Ethiopia*:

> "God created people and then dipped them in a bowl of water to cleanse them and the *first* came out clean and lily white. The next batch found the water a bit murkier and they came out not quite as clean, somewhat brownish. The *last* came when the water was nearly finished so they only managed to dip their palms and the soles of their feet!"

Nonsense, you may think. But put that to someone who has never seen anything else in life but a continuous portrayal of these inferior-superior roles. Then you would understand why to this date, some Africans still feel inadequate.

Africans in that society were the labourers on the farms and mines not for themselves but for their masters. They were told that their ways, culture and faith were barbaric and vain. There was a superior way that had been kindly brought by the master. Those who had the privilege to interact with the master soon realised that the master was always right and if he mistreated you, he was kind because, "Africans have no soul!"

They soon realised that the master possessed the wisdom of the gods! His second-hand clothes and leftovers made them see how kind he was. It was clear to everybody that all the people of the master's race were wise beyond words, educated and rich. It was also a given 'fact' that all the Africans were evil, ignorant and worthless.

As time went on, the brainwashing process continued when society's ideals used the master as the ultimate standard. Children ceased to play with clay models and wild fruit. They had white dolls and toys to aspire to. Slowly they were weaned from the artefacts of their culture. The scholars began to study books with pictures and stories reflecting foreign culture and lands far away. They soon mastered the language of the foreign masters and their own decayed and were lost.

Then they were trained to work for the master, only as assistants and general hands. For all this they were ever grateful. Thus, did the master-servant relationship evolve from one generation to another. Sadly, even today, the posh areas of our cities are still referred to as 'white'. Those with lots of money are *'my White man'*. All the beautiful things are 'white' and all that is bad and evil is 'of black people'.

This obviously is a serious case of stereotyping, but unfortunately it is still the basis of many an African society's mindset. This *is* Africa's problem. It is unfortunate because there are millions that mourn for the colonial era days, when they were still under white rule.

They argue that their nations were better governed and there weren't so many troubles as there are today. The sad truth is that these fellow Africans had so believed the myth of African inferiority that they never ventured out of colonisation of the mind. They also would rather not take the responsibility that comes with the freedom.

Shifting the mindset

The Bible records an interesting incident in Exodus 14:11-12;

> And they said unto Moses, because there were no graves in Egypt, has thou taken us away to die in the wilderness? Wherefore hast thou dealt thus with us, to carry us forth out of Egypt? Is this not the word that we did tell thee in Egypt saying, Let us alone that we may serve the Egyptians than that we should die in the wilderness.

Now, these people certainly were not longing for the slave drivers' whips that scarred their backs. Nor did they want to make bricks without straw. They had cried out to God about it in the first place! Two things are clear here. Firstly, they had lost their sense of identity as a free people. Their relationship with their former masters was "that we may *serve* the Egyptians." They were so brainwashed that they saw no life apart from the Egyptians. They claimed, "It is *better for us to serve* the Egyptians".

After 400 years of slavery, from generation to generation, they forgot that they were the children of Abraham, a special, chosen nation and saw themselves as Egyptian slaves. Their self-worth and peoplehood had been grievously distorted and their true identity lost. They needed a point of reference to redefine who they were. It is also striking to note that they were so Egypt-minded that they saw no future beyond slavery. There are four references to Egypt in those two verses!

The second thing is that they were not willing to take the responsibility that came with their freedom. They had presumed that it would be easy since it was God who initiated it. Reality checks along the way constantly brought them out of dreamland. Coming out of Egypt meant a need to take on their true identity and apply themselves to the conditions of the new experience. In a very similar way, these fellow Africans who wish they could rewind time are essentially trying to escape responsibility. True emancipation always takes a fight and a greater effort to be fully realised.

The pillars of society fell

The colonial era operated on manipulation and deceit. African land was taken in exchange for a few handguns, mirrors and sugar! The settlers came as "friends" and polite visitors who later became oppressors. One of their notorious methods was restructuring the society.

First to be disrupted was the family unit, which was also the place of learning and cultural focal point. Afterwards, the rest of society was easy to control. The new systems were imposed without consent and forced societies to change their ways of life too drastically, such that they lost a great deal that was of value to them and more so those distinctive characteristics that made them a people.

Racial segregation, violence and injustice were the tools that were used to establish the false perception of racial superiority of whites over Africans. With their land, cattle and freedom stolen from them, the societies were forced to conform to the new set up. Dissent was squashed by oppressive legislation and brutal force.

African people were packed in 'tribal lands', which were isolated arid places where there were persistent droughts where there were health hazards in form of tsetse fly and malaria. With the establishment of urban areas, industries came up and the men were taken to work. The women were not allowed in the city, neither those without authority from the oppressors and so the very soul of Africa died a slow and painful death.

The money that the men earned in the cities was later repossessed in form of taxes. Head tax, hut tax, dog tax, there was a tax for literally everything and that made sure that these men laboured for nothing all their life. Their children went to school in a system designed to offer them substandard education and train them to be servant of their white counterparts. The cases of such abuse are so many that we could write another book on them. But for now, our focus is to establish the root of this inferiority that has kept Africans playing the minor role in life.

As we have noted, the new systems of governance, education and the social structure were used to emphasise the white superiority and demean black people. This gradually crystallised into acceptable norms and standards. At school and home, at work, in society the African people were exposed to the superiority of whites and their inferiority in the racial continuum.

They learnt not to question the imbalances they saw every day. They knew that the land belonged to the white farmers and not them. They understood that they had no role or voice in the way they had to be governed. Their role was passive and input unnecessary. Over many years they finally accepted their secondary status as citizens in their own land.

Three

FALSE PERCEPTIONS

There are philosophies and premises upon which these oppressive fallacies were anchored. We look at some of these here. It is amazing that to date some of these sinister beliefs still hold millions in darkness. Actually, these are sometimes arguments by Africans who believe in African inferiority.

The Compensation Myth

This is an attempt to justify the oppression and atrocities committed against Africa by saying it brought more good than evil. Those people who subscribe to this myth point to the institutions set up by the colonisers such as hospitals, schools and cities as evidence.

They claim that Africa could still be in Stone Age had not the settlers bulldozed their way into our continent. Fair sounding, isn't it? It conveniently ignores that African resources were plundered by these unfair arrangements. How can you justify brutality and decimation of people with the buildings and institutions to which they don't even have access?

The freedom we now have was never handed to us but attained through a bloody struggle, without which we would still be slaves. The truth is that Africa was and continues to be looted by the colonialists who built their nations with our wealth. What we lost cannot compare a bit with what we got.

The Black man was cursed

This is a fatalistic pseudo-religious argument. It stems from the misinterpretation of the Biblical account in Genesis 9 where Noah cursed Canaan the son of Ham, one of his three sons. Ham discovered his father in a drunken state of undress and went out to tell his two brothers who responded by covering their father. Upon waking up from his drunken stupor Noah said:

> "Cursed be Canaan, A servant of servants shall he be unto his brethren." (9v25).

Now, there are several factors that discount the use of this scripture as a basis for the advancement of the myth that black people are a cursed race. Firstly, in verse 1 of the same chapter we read *"And God blessed Noah and his sons..."* Now that God blessed them, a curse surely would not stick as Balaam's words say, "How I curse whom God has not cursed? Or how shall I defy whom God has not defiled" (Numbers 23v8) Noah's curse could not overshadow God's blessing on Ham. Besides, the curse was not directed at him but Canaan and if you trace the genealogy further in chapter 10 it reveals that the African people came through the line of Cush not Canaan. The NIV Study Bible commentary makes this interesting note on the verse;

> "This statement cannot be used to justify the enslavement of blacks since those who were cursed were Canaanites who were Caucasian."

Secondly, there is no biblical basis for the assertion. This incident is an isolated family event. The curse is an angry outburst by a father who shamed himself before his son while drunk and does not necessarily warrant God's backing. Nowhere beyond this incident is the issue raised either in reference or theologically.

The Dark Continent

At the turn of the 19th century, European leaders convened the infamous Berlin Conference, during what was to be called the 'Scramble for Africa.' They parcelled Africa among themselves. This period saw massive importation of European values and culture into Africa and the simultaneous looting of precious African resources. As a result, Africa's own beauty and identity was to be forever marred.

African civilisation, economies and political kingdoms were crashed and for the first time Africans became 'black' and the colonisers were 'white.' Ironically, that was also to refer to the condition and heart and mind. Slavery was born and untold massacres and most crude atrocities were carried out on unsuspecting communities, families and innocent victims. Before long the 'whites' were masters and 'blacks' slaves. Our cultures and systems were replaced by 'more civilised' European alternatives. Even our names and languages were termed *vernacular*.

Our ideals soon became European as all that was ours, we were told to discard. It has been over a century, but we seem to have nearly lost our entire heritage. We became victims of massive cultural identity corruption. The mere recounting of these will grieve any African heart. It is sadder to see our generations and children still looking up to 'white' ideals.

Deceptive education

There was a deceptive hole in the education that we got as it converted us from our *African-ness*. It provided us with no heroes or ideals that are our own. It still perpetuates the myth that persuaded our fathers to believe that white oppression was a blessing.

Our history depicts us as normal human beings who lived in warm, loving and God-fearing communities. Listen to the songs of Africa, they are celebratory, they speak of family and community, they praise God and reveal our awareness of other people.

African societies in pre-colonial times were characterised with social progress, political establishments and stable economic systems and excellence in every field imaginable. Relationships and values have always been central as reflected in the family structure, which was all-inclusive and well structured. It is therefore a false claim that the continent was dark and the coming of the colonisers enlightened us.

People who subscribe to this fallacy tend to think that the colonialists were representative of their societies in totality. They have not examined the societies of the 'superior race' and experienced the vice and evil thereof. They do not realise that all men are the same and that *black* and *white* are a creation of colonialism.

What did Africans invent?

Some people have devised the myth of invention. They claim that whites have invented so many things and that proves that they are better endowed intellectually. The selectivity of this claim betrays its foolishness.

Firstly, the conception of ideas is based on needs. It is the needs that determine the invention of things. This myth fails to take into cognisance that each people group has invented methods and products that made their lives simpler and objectives achievable.

Secondly, the myth assumes that technology is only to be defined in terms of westernised concepts such as cars and computers. A San man and his family who survive daily life with ease in the Kalahari with only a bow and arrows and desert intelligence is far better off than an outsider who may die in a short while if his 4x4 vehicle broke down in the same desert environment. The islanders who crossed the seas without radar or compass in simple vessels possessed great intelligence and scientific understanding. Technology as a concept must be understood contextually.

Yet another factor that the *technology myth* leaves out is that there are millions of inventions by Africans in modern technology. It only takes one to read the scientific journals or a simple Google search to find that inventing did not stop with the wheel or the electric bulb!

Is Africa independent?

When freedom from colonialism came in most of Africa, people were introduced to the concept that Government was omnipotent and so rich, *he* would build them houses, roads, cater for their health needs, feed and send their children to school and keep them happy forever. Indeed, many new governments managed to sort out some of the imbalances that the colonial era had created by providing as much as they could, opportunities for education and other primary needs such as health and employment.

But it is unrealistic for a whole nation to sit with folded hands and make demands on their government as if it could work magic. No government can be effective without the active participation and support of its people. This perception portrays the government as an entity that resides in the government offices and institutions, ready to spend a fortune on anyone who comes knocking on its door!

Frederic Bastic, an economist, said of the government:

> 'Government is the great fiction through which everybody endeavours to live at the expense of everyone else'.

We have seen gross abuse of public property from junior officers to executives and the general public. All do so because they believe that somehow there is an inexhaustible mine of resources. Another economist, John S. Coleman adds the following point:

> 'The point to remember is that what the government gives it must first take away.'

It is true therefore that if we are to make any demands on our governments we must first contribute. Many people worry and change their leaders whom they blame for incompetence. It may be suggested however, that in most instances it is a case of citizen incompetence! Government just cannot function without active participation of the people in all spheres and sectors. Independence was not meant to liberate us from working for a living, rather from working for others!

All of us have experienced the insufficient and half-hearted and at times abusive service at government offices. This is the very evidence of the blanket misconception that it does not matter how we handle our jobs as long as we get paid.

But being paid for not doing what you should, is taking from government without contributing and this is short-changing everyone else. This phenomenon is particularly widespread in the civil service sector where output is not easily quantifiable. Governments lose millions in revenue because of irresponsible staff. They are not incompetent because they have been trained to do their jobs, but they are irresponsible because they refuse to do it.

This does not apply to the public sector alone. Even the private and informal sectors suffer too. We have seen communities that are so addicted to hand-outs that they will not work! Ideally, all able minded and bodied people should not be accepted for donated foodstuffs. This concept has created lazy and over-dependent people, thus killing the work ethic in us. No wonder we don't seem to make much progress.

We are so guided by the 8am – 5pm syndrome that nobody wants to volunteer anything. We have seen people flock into programs hoping to make a quick buck and later quit because there was hard work involved. Dr Warren Bennis once wrote that young people no longer dream of going to the moon or making a better mousetrap, but that they dream of money. It is sad to see this negative attitude of money-driveness grip our nations.

Corruption

The love of money breeds corruption. We are not strangers to corruption in our society where people illegitimately, try to squeeze something out of us for services they should render. Sometimes in the most unorthodox of ways!

Whenever one engages in corrupt activities, they are casting off their part of the corporate responsibility that we share as citizens of a nation. In essence, they are breaching a contract and selfishly letting us all down.

Some argue that corruption in their part of the world has reached incorrigible levels. It is possible to feel overwhelmed by the cancerous pervasiveness, but change *is* possible! One person can start a chain of positive action and literally change the course of a nation.

However, it starts with a decision. If you are in service, decide to serve with your heart. If you work, do it with all your effort. If you are in the informal sector, decide not to stay there forever! We can change our nations by changing ourselves first. We must substitute negative behaviour and thinking with positive.

There are no better words to express this than those of Paul writing to the Christians at Ephesus;

> He who has been stealing must steal no longer, but must work doing something useful with his own hands and mind that he may have something to share with those in need (Eph 4v28)

Wasted Potential

Responsibility for our continent has met a few hurdles that are a residue of the previous eras. These are in form of impeding mental concepts, which naturally put a limit to our estimation of our capacity. Sheer laziness and a give-me-give-me attitude have also severely crippled us.

Dr. Myles Munroe once said the richest place in the world is the cemetery! Because there lies all that should have been but never became. It is frightening sometimes to imagine how much African potential is going to waste on a daily basis.

In our daily interaction with our environment, with our creative minds we must seek to discover new ways and approaches to life. Kent Ruth wrote so strikingly accurate:

> 'Man can live without air for a few minutes, without water for about two weeks, without food for about two months and without a new thought for years on end.'

This is very true especially when one considers our sometimes, pathetic approach to life. We are trained to look for a job, so we leave our fate to other people. We blame life for dealing us a harsh blow. The days of waiting for the right time are over. We must teach ourselves to seek, seize and even create opportunity!

In the olden days, one was apprenticed from a very early stage and as they matured, their contribution became more significant and independent. There was no waiting to be creative. Modern Africa has however brought us up feeling inadequate and unqualified to make tangible inputs into society. So, we strive to obtain 'the papers' before we do anything.

We tend to believe that the criteria used by employers and institutions, as their 'minimum requirements' is also a measure for all of life! Nothing could be further from the truth. Our societies are so 'minimum requirements' conscious that we bury our talents and feel sorry for ourselves all our lives. We don't need a high school certificate to make our lives count! Neither do we need a university degree to be successful in life.

We are creative beings. Our creativity is internal rather than induced. Each person has a great capacity to be great and excel. Deep within us we have what it takes to live a fulfilling life. We have skills and capabilities lying there on the inside. We are not validated by academic achievements as important as they may be. We have value in our unique individuality and there is a God-given route to excellence waiting to be explored. If we reach in and tap into that creativity, we may be amazed how much we have got.

Conclusion

In this first part, we drew our attention to the rich historic heritage that Africa has. It is in understanding this that we can look at our present status and chart an effective plan for our future. It is in acknowledging both our good and bad that we can honestly seek a better future.

Our identity and roots are of ultimate importance if we will contribute effectively to the legacy of our fathers and to the good of our children. We cannot afford to mourn the effect of our negative experiences forever. Rather, they should inspire us to seek our true potential and live it out to the benefit of the world.

Apart from the negative political heritage, Africa has also emerged with good things from the past era. This includes the possession and control of that which our fathers' sweat and blood produced. Political freedom came with the numerous rights and privileges. The infrastructure, which included industries, in some cases, thriving economies and automatic membership into the international community. We also inherited education and our dignity was restored as each country became sovereign and self-governing.

Political freedom however was not all there was. Embracing it was a signature to fulfil the responsibilities thereof. Africa received a big basket that contained economies, political systems, cultures international ties, natural resources and the aspirations of the masses.

It was up to the people themselves to decide what they wanted to do with it. This tremendous responsibility is probably one of the most important elements of Africa's heritage. The responsibility to manage the Big Basket ensuring the progress of the continent from a negative era into the future that has a progressive and fulfilling nature.

Part 2

THE EVOLUTION OF A CONTINENT

Four

MODERN AFRICA

This era starts during the colonial and extends into the post-colonial period. The rise of the politically fragmented content divided primarily on the basis of people groups, agricultural regions and natural resources. These were predominantly determined by the colonial powers. The post-colonial era brought a new identity to Africa.

It was the culmination of the dream of Nationalistic pride and independence. This was the era of black rule. Needless to say, it was also an era of optimism and high hopes. One by one and with help from others, the African states became independent. Beginning in Ghana in 1963 until 1994, the African people have hoped and prayed and struggled.

Nkrumah of Ghana, a man who is regarded as the father of the nationalistic movement once said; "Seek ye first the political kingdom and everything else shall follow." This sufficed as the war cry for mass mobilisation. Unfortunately, as many of our postcolonial governments have come to realise, political independence is not everything.

The economic, religious, social and cultural independence is equally important. The change of political ideology should be accompanied by economic empowerment. Each of these freedoms is equally important. Let us examine each of these freedom concepts as they have been experienced in modern Africa.

Political Freedom

This refers to all forms of governance of society and the creation of a national identity of a people. Of primary concern was legislation, national institutions and socio-economic progress. Having been fed up with the oppressive rule of the colonialists, dissenting voices began to arise among the ranks of the oppressed. Sooner the armed struggle to overthrow the status quo began.

Many people died in combat, but their lives they counted unworthy for the liberation of their fellow countrymen. In some African countries, we see a bad tendency to forget these heroes or restrict the honour to just a few politicians. Many however honour them and always seek to remind their children and themselves the importance of the price paid for the freedom they now enjoy.

This era came with new flags and national anthems that would be constant reminders of the dark past and what we hope for in the future. The new language was peace and prosperity. African leaders were inaugurated and doors were opened for the voice of the masses to be heard. In truth, those were to be the sweetest years in the history of many African nations.

Soon the honeymoon would give way to the harsh reality that political freedom alone was inadequate. Some of the new leaders quickly became oppressors themselves. They forgot to give people their land back or to fulfil the promises that they made during their election campaigns. This was the root of the post-independence disillusionment of our freedom.

Greedy pursuit of selfish gratification, corruption and tyranny saw the rise of the dictatorships, looting of national resources and the so-called civil wars. This phenomenon has led to the ruined image of the African continent. It is sad that future generations will bear this burden for many years to come. However, some leaders were positive. They built schools, hospitals and put a lot of infrastructure in place. They established democratic governments and stepped down to allow others take over. It is a sad truth that only a few can claim this credit. But they are there!

One of the reasons for the political problems in Africa is that we have not developed much in the other areas of life. We got politics and ran off with it without much thought given to what we call the civic elements of our nations. The civic includes religious, cultural and social aspects of our lives. The political orientation discussed above pays too much attention to the political identity of a nation. So, they invest in their defence, foreign affairs and a costly international image rather than in those things that improve the individual citizen so he can be a better and proud participant in his or her country's life.

Economic Freedom

The mistake that the successive post-independence governments in Africa have made has been their failure to implement effective economic policies. It is not a lie that for most independent African States, the economy is still in the hands of the former colonialists. They own the industries, they own all the good land; they own all the resource, the mines, forests, seas and wildlife. In Zimbabwe, South Africa, Malawi, Kenya and many places, we still have landless people who are referred to as squatters. Actually, in Zimbabwe by the year 2000, twenty years after independence, nearly 90% of all the fertile land belonged to about 4 000 white farmers, who could choose to share it with the black majority or not. In fact, they chose the latter.

As you might be aware, economic empowerment goes with education, but access to resources is the more important issue. Nigeria, a nation well-endowed with resources including oil and very intelligent and able human resources, has been consistently destabilised yet the big oil names still make millions. A single family owns Southern Africa's diamonds and its gold; gas and platinum reserves still belong to non-Africans. The war in Angola went on for nearly 30 years, but their diamonds are still being mined and sold by non-Angolans.

The grasp of the economic means has been ever elusive for African people despite our education and competence; we still have no room in the making of money. Notwithstanding, there are a lot of Africans who have risen to the highest levels of the economic network and are dedicated to empowering fellow Africans. This is very important because without economic means there is no chance for progress. Political freedom without the economic freedom is a fraud.

Black Economic Empowerment

This is a very popular concept with many African governments. It served mainly as an attempt to rejuvenate the failing or failed economies. It was a realisation that there was need for a more equitable distribution of economic resources. The economic take-over proved catastrophic when the African business leaders without adequate training and experience just couldn't steer the economy to expected levels. More so the sabotage by their white counterparts was not a minor issue. The Black Economic Empowerment (BEE) concept seeks to redress the situation by equipping the majority of the population to be major stakeholders in the economy. Empowerment encompasses, knowledge, skills, decision-making, access to resources and above all dignity and fair treatment.

BEE is not to be confused with a mere swapping of management roles with whites or a wee opening at the top. It must afford each player an opportunity that is proportional to their capacity to contribute into and benefit from the economy. It should also include the continuous attempt to improve their capacity to its optimum.

This brilliant concept has failed to provide a meaningful transformation in the sectors of the economy of many African states. This, often as a result of the flagging political will as well as limited access to economic resources. Empowerment implies independence, power and influence. However, in most cases the results have been the enrichment of a few black top dogs and poverty for the rest of the people.

Poverty is one of Africa's major challenges. BEE is supposed to address the question of access to and ownership of the economic means by black people. This is a task that cannot be realised through the change of legislation alone. The change of legislation should be seen as the key that opens the once blockaded areas so that the opportunities that we never had may be realised. It calls for the rise of an African entrepreneur who thinks and measures him or herself with a positive scale. Indeed, governments will have to do something to enable their people to catch up and be equipped with the necessary skills to be competent. And of course, there is a long way to go, but the time is now!

Black economic empowerment is more than levelling the playing field. It should of necessity involve the enabling of the Africans to do for themselves what they have been doing for others. This is more a psychological issue than a political one. It is of utter importance that the re-education process begins if the opportunities that are created by legislation are to be fully realised by our people. This is not an issue of government or NGO-sponsored seminars!

We make a grievous mistake to make our lives and the progress of our societies the responsibility of a few people. Empowerment is incomplete if it only emancipates a few. It should be pursued as an ideal for the good of all. The responsibility of uplifting our communities and countries is everyone's, just as was the liberation from colonial domination. The African post-colonial era has produced much despondency because the sooner we got our 'freedom' we forgot about the *ideals* that we fought for in the first place!

Economic empowerment is about a people discovering their potential and working hard to turn the way it is to what it should be! Each one of us must contribute. The quest is to encourage independent thinking and a creative spirit that exists within each one of us for the good of all.

The few ultra-rich individuals and highfliers are not living the "African Dream" on our behalf. Each person must get their own slice of the cake! If all we do is admire or envy them, then their success is irrelevant to us. Success is not necessarily measured in millions but certainly in the ability to live a decent life and access to life's basic necessities. This is still a distant dream for many African communities.

Five

GOVERNANCE ISSUES

One of the most sensational cases in the early history of the new millennium was the Zimbabwean Land Question. It was the cause of a great confusion for those watching from the side-lines and yet a duel of life and death for those involved in the struggle.

On one side, the government of Robert Mugabe was compulsorily acquiring farming land for resettling the local population who had been deprived of the land since the 1890's. On the other hand, the British government of Tony Blair accused Mugabe of lawlessness and human rights abuses.

The battle left the diplomatic halls to the farms and then to the media and even to the cricket pitch! (The British team boycotted the 2003 ICC Cricket World Cup games held in Zimbabwe). This was seen as a politically motivated act of trying to 'get at Mugabe.' One would however want to get to the point of conflict. Why this whole fray?

The Land Question

> "We are a poor people. All we have is our land...if you take our land from us, then we are nothing."

This was one of many of President Mugabe's key lines on the conflict between his Government and the British. He took his crusade to all the international platforms he could get! In the process, he became a hero and villain depending on your side!

In the 1890s the first of the British settlers arrived in the land beyond the Limpopo River having advanced from the coastal areas towards the interior. The mission of the settlers was conquest. They had a plan all worked out to take this virgin land and its resources for the crown.

At the head of this campaign was the man Cecil John Rhodes after whom the central interior was to be named, *Rhodesia*. When the local people realised that these 'visitors' had sinister motives, they put up a brave fight, but they were to be outwitted by the invaders. The land, which was the basis of their livelihood, was eventually taken away and they were relocated to arid and uninhabitable areas. Their livestock was also taken from them and they became slaves in their own land.

There is historic evidence as well as documents to verify these facts. For most of the 20th century, successive African generations tried to cope with the new arrangement. However, a time came when the people decided to join forces to regain their land. After a bitter war of nearly 30 years the struggle brought independence from Britain. Rhodesia became Zimbabwe in 1980. This was a negotiated settlement from the long-drawn Lancaster House Conference. Something noteworthy was the conditional clause on the land issue that was attached to the independence deal.

The white farmers/landowners were to be guaranteed a ten-year free tenure of the land. These constituted just about 4000 whites that owned literally all the best farmland. At the end of the period the land was to be acquired by the government for redistribution on what was termed the *'willing buyer-willing seller'* method. Unfortunately, after 10 years there were no willing sellers! So, the Zimbabwean people waited another 10 years. Then some 'willing' sellers were claiming exorbitant prices for the soil they had farmed for an extra ten free years!

A land conference held in Harare failed dismally as the British incumbent government reneged on all responsibility as stated in the Lancaster House Agreement. Mugabe's government was under pressure ahead of the 2000 elections. The government then gave 'permission' to seize the land from the white farmers. Thus, began the struggle for life on the farms. Many opponents of the land reform argue that the Mugabe government was abusing human rights by taking the land from the white farmers. The proponents respond by asking if there were no human rights when their forefathers were displaced.

It is important to note two things at this stage. Firstly, that the 'grace' period, which was doubled, had expired. Secondly, for an ordinary Zimbabwean to own a fertile piece of land is a matter of life and death, let alone making a profit from the land. Another spanner in the works was the arrogance of the white Commercial Farmers' Union, which refused to negotiate an amicable settlement with the government. The disastrous consequences of the land reform program in Zimbabwe were compounded by the political nature of the issue.

Sadly, the land issue is not exclusive to Zimbabwe. Other African countries are yet to fight their own struggles to regain their land. Many African states still have a vast acreage under white ownership. The white farmers supposedly possess exclusive expertise in the tillage of the land and so assume the sole responsibility of 'feeding the nation.'

It is so in Kenya, South Africa, Malawi, Zambia and the rest of Africa. One wonders why the black people are unable to feed themselves when it is actually them who till the land and produce the food. Of course, there is a very subtle irony in this. The post-colonial inequity with regard to the land is a glaring misnomer. The land is a heritage from God to a people and no one has a right to take it away from them by force or trickery! African land belongs to the Africans and no one else must lay claim to its ownership except the African people.

What is ours?

Sometimes one wonders what the liberation struggle brought for Africa besides the days we celebrate and of course a bit of the life we have so idealised that our former oppressors lived. The mineral rights, the wildlife, the factories and the land still technically belong to the former colonialists! What then is ours?

These are sad but true realities that every African must ask and insist on getting answers to. Our fathers died and left us nothing. We fought hard to put an end to oppression and finally when we have thrown off the yoke of slavery, we discover that we have nothing to pass on to our children!

With the rise of an organised Africa, one has hope that we will be able to break free from this the exploitative alliances with the rest of the world. It is suspicious that African countries go up in smoke, yet the multinational corporations of the West go on with their day-to-day operations. Could one be wrong to suspect that they have something to do with these disturbances? Take Nigeria for instance. For many decades, Muslim military leaders ruled Nigeria but never suggested the introduction of the *sharia law* as the law of the land. However, when the new democracy showed up and Nigeria moved towards stability the violence and intolerance erupted in 2002.

The Democratic Republic of Congo is another example. When Mobutu Seseseko ruled that country, the Western interests were safe and the country was stagnant. When the rebel movements ousted the dictator, a new order was established and that meant the change of ownership of mineral rights and that was the beginning of the war without end. Most people believe that African leaders have involved themselves in the conspiracy against their own people.

Over the centuries the African people have been oppressed in this same way of dividing them and the enticement of their leaders to sell their souls for money. It always turns out to be a vain dream at the end of one's life as many have realised too late. The call to leadership in Africa is a very sacred call because unlike in the other places it is a duel for the very soul of the African people. It is of importance therefore that any leader at any level must make a commitment to defend the sovereignty of this beautiful land from external control regardless whether it's from Washington, Paris or Beijing.

God of Africa?

Our world has become increasingly scornful of religion and the very belief in God. With the rise of multiculturalism, multifaithism has also come up. Africa like the rest of the world has nearly lost her ties with deity.

There are two major misconceptions about African faith that must be pointed out and repudiated. First, Africa is *not* multi-theistic. Research and tradition provide evidence that Africa has always believed in the one God, the Creator, the God of Heaven, the maker of all things and the Great-Great One. The way to this God was not readily known but his power and greatness were acknowledged. Here is enshrined the relevance of the Christian faith. In declaring the one whom Africa worshiped without knowledge for many generations.

The second misconception is that Christianity is neo-colonialist in nature. This is not true, as we shall see later. The Christian faith played a very important role in the emancipation of the African people from the oppressive domination by colonialists. The Christian teaching is that all men are equal before God and are all entitled to the basic rights as dignified citizens of the world that He created. In fact, the diversity of our appearances and geographic locations are his very design to fulfil his purpose. In Acts 10v34-35, Peter in realisation proclaims;

> "that God does not show favouritism, but accepts men from every nation..."

God and Governance

The rise of the idea of secular democracy has afforded us the most elaborate of freedoms, even the freedom to choose whether to worship God or not! Communism believed in the power of the state. Socialism advocated for humanistic co-operation. Capitalism believes in the power of the individual. Very few nations except those that are declared Islamic states bother to promote religion.

Faith has become a topical issue. The USA, for instance, is a declared 'Christian' nation whose foundations were based on biblical principles. However, the same nation has come so low that it is even against the law to pray in the school or talk about one's faith in public media! The anti-God movement is strong and fiercely opposed to the Judeo-Christian tradition. Thus, atheistic secularism thrives using the institutions of democracy.

As societies become affluent, more 'educated' and sophisticated, they seem to find less and less need for God. Or so have they become deluded. However, there are wide cracks showing that these nations need God more than before. Psalm 53v10-12 says:

> The Lord foils the plans of the nations; He thwarts the purposes of the peoples. But the plans of the Lord stand firm forever, the purposes of his heart through all generations. Blessed is the nation whose God is the Lord...

Blessedness is one state that any nation should promote and pursue. After all, the Bible declares that;

> Righteousness exalts a nation and sin is a reproach to any people. (Prov 14v34)

A nation that seeks to promote righteousness shall be blessed. Righteousness not in terms of low crime levels or a record of hospitality to tourists! Rather, a commitment to the fear and worship of God. Where people value the moral laws of God and build homes and raise their children in the ways of holiness. Where people demonstrate a sense of understanding of the rulership of God over their lives and responsibility in the way they live with each other.

The psalmist King David of Israel himself would further reiterate from his experience in the 144th Psalm:

> Then our sons in their youth will be like well-nurtured plants and our daughters will be like pillars carved to adorn a palace. Our barns will be filled with every kind of provision. Our sheep will increase by thousands, by tens of thousands in our fields; our oxen will draw heavy loads. There will be no breaching of walls, no going into captivity, no cry of distress in our streets. Blessed are the people of whom this is true. (v12-15)

In very simple terms, the nation whose God is *not* the Lord shall not be blessed. Deductively therefore, the opposite of the blessings listed here, shall happen to it. It is historically true that if a nation ignores God, its peril is certain but if it acknowledges him, the blessing is guaranteed. When the apostle Paul wrote to the Roman Christians, he mentioned some of the terrible consequences of having nothing to do with God.

> Although they knew God, they neither glorified him as God nor gave thanks to Him. But their thinking became futile and their foolish hearts were darkened. Although they claimed to be wise, they became fools and exchanged the glory of the immortal God for images.... Therefore God gave them over to the sinful desires of their hearts, to sexual impurity for the degrading of their bodies with one another. They exchanged the truth of God for a lie and served created things rather than the creator... Because of this God gave them over to shameful lusts. Even their women exchanged natural relations for unnatural ones. In the same way also men abandoned natural relations with women...Furthermore, since they did not think it worthwhile to retain the knowledge of God, he gave them over to a depraved mind to do what ought not to be done.

This is a very sad passage of scripture, yet it mirrors the actual state of many a nation today, where the God of the Bible is an optional extra for a few 'fundamentalists.' But the nation that serves God shall be blessed. Some African states are not far off from this kind of God forsakenness!

Promoting righteousness

We should note here that the God of the Bible is the God of Africa-and the whole world. We had been lost to him but he has revealed himself to us through his Son Jesus Christ who died on the cross to pay the penalty of our sin and rose again from the dead, so that we might have eternal relationship with him when we believe. Previously we were groping around with puzzling clues and traditions, but now he has opened a new and living way for us.

> For God so loved the world that he gave us his only begotten son that whosoever shall believe in him shall not perish but shall have eternal life. (John 3v16)

Jesus himself declared;

> "I am the way, the truth and the life. No one comes to the Father except by me." (John 14v 6)

Jesus is the distinction between the Christian faith and all other faiths. He is the *person* upon whom the faith is based and endures. As scripture reveals he is the only one that has claimed and proved that he can regenerate a human heart. Jesus is the only one who can bring a real relationship between God and man.

Paul said it so clearly to the Greek philosophers in Athens:

> I even found an inscription: TO AN UNKNOWN GOD. Now what you worship as something unknown I am going to proclaim to you. (Acts 17v23).

He went on to explain how God had planned it such that Jesus would reveal him to all men. Unfortunately, the signs of ungodliness are glaring at us in our day-to-day lives. Righteousness is trampled and the so-called 'democratic' constitutions, laws and bylaws overpower truth. We have the courts that preserve our rights - rights even to expel God from our lives. And what do we get for our effort? Violence, terrorism, AIDS, crime and worse cases of inhumanity. Are we surprised? We shouldn't be, because righteousness exalts a nation but sin is a disgrace to any people. (Prov 14v34) and the nation whose God is the Lord shall be blessed.

Each God-fearing African should make a commitment to promote righteousness in their nation, be it at home, school or workplace. Let us influence our environment and our people for good. Those in leadership positions of authority should make an effort to promote righteousness and the fear of God over our nations. Then shall we see God's blessing upon our continent.

Warning Rulers

The nation was Egypt, a leading kingdom with great military power and a legacy of rich and powerful rulers-the Pharaohs. With a rapidly advancing agricultural technology and superb infrastructure, they also had revolutionary literary and cultural developments. They were the centre of world trade and a million-strong slave labour workforce. What more could a nation want?

Astrology and secret sciences and a host of gods were enough for the faith needs of Egypt-until the God of heaven showed up and demanded freedom for the slaves. "Who is the Lord that I should obey him and let Israel go? I do not know the Lord and I will not let Israel go", declared Pharaoh. But after a few encounters with the Lord God of heaven, he was not only willing to let Israel go but he actually drove them away!

Rebellious nations only invite the wrath of God upon themselves. The lesson that Egypt learnt was that it is important to co-operate with God and if a nation does not recognise God; it is to their own hurt.

A King in the meadows!
Several hundred years later, a new superpower had emerged and dictated the rules for every nation under heaven. Babylon was the name. God described them in his conversation with the prophet Habakkuk;

> I am raising up the Babylonians, that ruthless and impetuous people...They are a feared and dreaded people they are a law to themselves and promote their honour...they gather prisoners like sand, they deride kings and scoff at rulers. They laugh at fortified cities ...guilty men whose own strength is their God (Hab 1v6-11).

Babylon was a great nation and too powerful for any other to challenge them. But they really had a big problem. They had no God. The book of Daniel in particular reveals that their worship was so erratic they worshipped golden images and various other gods. Sometimes they would substitute these with the king on temporary basis! The scripture quoted above indicates God's opinion of them; 'guilty men whose own strength is their god'.

After their military campaign where they destroyed the temple and city of the famed God of Israel, they believed they owed no God any worship. But God had his people among them. He visited the king Nebuchadnezzar in a perplexing dream. When the man had come to his wits' end; God sent his servant and explained its meaning. In chapter 2v45 we read the result:

> Then king Nebuchadnezzar fell prostrate before Daniel and ordered that an offering and incense be presented to him. The king said to Daniel, surely your God is the God of gods and the lord of kings...'

Unfortunately, the king was a slow learner and he soon forgot the 'God of gods' and built an image for all his people to worship. God however wasn't through with him yet. When he rescued his servants from the king's fiery furnace, which was punishment for refusing to bow down before this image, he decreed total destruction to anyone 'who says anything against the God of Shadrech, Meshach and Abednego.' That sounds like the 'freedom of worship' clause of our democracy. Just do not disturb someone when they worship their own god. They have a right to worship whoever and however they choose to.

God however is not a democrat. He is autocratic. He either rules or he does not. There are no 50/50 commitments to him. He wants to rule over our nations. Kings rule in his stead and it is him that appoints and removes them at will. There is no power sharing with God! A king or ruler who does not acknowledge God is foolish. So was king Nebuchadnezzar when he boasted himself;

> Is not this the great Babylon I have built as the royal residence, by my power and the glory of my majesty? While the words were still in his lips, God's judgement was pronounced. Your royal authority has been taken from you. You will be driven away from people and you shall live with the wild animals. You will eat grass like cattle. Seven [years] shall pass by for you until you acknowledge that the most high is sovereign over the kingdoms of men and gives them to anyone he wishes. (v31-32).

When this happened, the king became a changed man and his speech reflects it in verses 34-37. God was still not through with the nation. The next king, Belshazzar suffered the consequences of failing to honour God when the finger of God wrote on the wall that the days of his rule had instantly expired. *'MENE MENE TEKEL UPARSIN'* was the message from God. It was Darius the next king who after seeing the triumph of the God of Daniel finally declared:

> I issue a decree that in every part of my kingdom people must fear and revere the God of Daniel. And this decree was to remain in accordance with the law of the Medes and Persians, which cannot be repealed. (6v26.)

Hence the next king after him, upheld it and Cyrus ordered the return of the Jewish exiles and ordered the rebuilding of the temple and city of Jerusalem. The records are in the biblical books of Ezra and Nehemiah.

In summary, these cases prove three points. Firstly, God rules and if acknowledged by a nation; that nation shall be blessed. Secondly, righteousness is the basis of the blessedness of the nation and God will use individuals who are committed to him. And finally, a nation *can* worship God through Jesus Christ and in true righteousness for in him is it found. In some parts of Africa, Jesus has always been absent or viewed as an optional extra. The belief that our ancestors and goodness are enough is a deception. So is the trust in our host of 'prophets' of whom the continent is now awash. Jesus Christ should be central to our faith and pursuit of the God whom our fathers worshipped in fear and uncertainty. Through him, every nation is called because:

> "Neither is salvation in any other, for there is no other name under heaven given among man by which we might be saved" (Act4v12)

Part 3

AFRICA TODAY

Six

REORGANISING THE PEOPLE

We have looked at the political and religious elements of modern Africa, but that is not all there is to our problem. Our greatest need is to adapt to the changes in our environment as quickly as possible without changing our basic defining elements such as cultural heritage, faith in God and freedom.

The global community

Twenty-first century Africa is a paradox of two fronts. On one side is highly sophisticated ultra-modern world that is not different from the so-called developed world - the city. Lagos, Johannesburg, Nairobi, Harare, Kinshasa, Maputo and many others that have put Africa on the international map.

They are fully equipped with their restaurants, neon lights, sophisticated communication networks, traffic jams and a host of other metropolitan frills. Only a few kilometres away from the giant cities are communities that are a century or two behind. A greater part of Africa's population is to be found here as rural peasant farmers, landless squatters, farm labourers etc. Their links to the outside world are very limited. These communities have emerged at a snail's pace, but unfortunately without them Africa will not go very far. The axiom is fulfilled that; 'You are as fast as the slowest among you.'

Africa has many genuine reasons for her lag behind the rest of the world. We have evidence that justifies that we could be better off than what we are. Unfortunately, that will not guarantee us any progress, nor will it improve our state at all. The only way for us is to catch up with the rest. Surely that means we must run faster and longer, but that is the way to go. Collaboration is an important foundation to an effective catch-up strategy.

The African society

African communities have two advantages that are essential for progress. The first is their communal orientation. From many years ago, the life of any nation has depended on each individual's responsible contribution to the welfare of the whole. The *Harambe* system in Kenya has seen massive community-oriented development. This is a development initiated by locals who share their resources with their community.

Undoubtedly, Nigeria is Africa's powerhouse both in natural and human resources. Nigerians everywhere are symbolic of determination and hard work that exist in Africa (and sadly lead in many other unorthodox activities too!). Truly, many other Africans are achieving excellence in a wide range of fields in life.

African communities were governed by a hierarchy of leadership structures with a strong grassroots engagement. These structures were more value based than legal. A leader was accountable to the people as much as they were to him or her. The Zulu saying *"Inkosi yinkosi ngabantu"* literally means "A king is king because of the people."

Even when the leadership structures emerged led by nationalist politicians, they received the same status their predecessors were given. They were expected to serve. There has always been collaboration between the two. In some parts though, the role of traditional leadership has become a little more than figurehead. Most of us in Africa however still answer to dual authority i.e. the village Chief and the elected government.

The African Union

There has been a steering in certain parts of Africa in recent times. Major developments have taken place in all spheres of life. Great spiritual, business and political leaders and entrepreneurs have emerged from the continent. There are increasing efforts to collaborate with greater efficiency and interdependence than during the nationalistic era.

The AU and other regional bodies are signs of our time. These institutions initiated and managed by Africans have sought to consolidate our continental structure. These are indicators of our continent's maturity and competence in the context of 21st Century global developments. Slow indeed, but sure! Not working effectively, but nonetheless existent.

The African Renaissance

This is a vision of Africa renewed and regenerated. It is a transformation of society right through its profile. It focuses on helping people find their identity, analyse their circumstances effectively and plan their future purposefully. This certainly is a long process characterised by pain and effort. However, it has rewards and benefits comparable to none. The process is three-fold.

First, we must redress our past. To figure out where we are and where we are going, we must know where we come from. The second step will be to thoughtfully analyse our current circumstances.

We have an abundance of commentary and daily experiences to give us an accurate picture of African realities. Finally, we need to formulate a plan for the future. We must visualise the Africa we want and then begin to work towards it.

Dealing with the Past

Every society must grow and develop holistically. The colonial era programmed us to look at life in distinct compartmentalised categories. As already mentioned above, we have a different hat for everything from politics, to religion to family and work. This is not how life is lived though. Life tends to come in an integrated fashion. Sadly, millions of Africans from preschool to professors are being and have been trained this way.

Healing the wounds

To change this, we must look at our past and determine which aspects of our history must be restored and reinforced. Herein lies our future. Among the African countries the past is still a sealed can of worms. Many cases of injustice and violation of rights have been consistently swept under the carpet in a blind pursuit of the so-called reconciliation.

Colonial and post-colonial atrocities have been ignored and trivialised. There has been a lot emphasis of peace *over* justice. However, there cannot be any justice without restitution. Africa's past is that of pain and abuse. As nations and a continent, we cannot make the kind of progress that we desire unless we face our past and have issues there redressed.

There are issues of political violence. Too many African conflicts are mediated with foreign interests and often settlements are reached hurriedly without addressing the real issues. The results are wars without end. Warring parties are blackmailed and cajoled into ostentatious compromise deals.

The second crucial element is that of socio-economic reform. Indigenisation has been offered as a viable process to ensure the transfer of wealth and equitable distribution of the economic means. Unfortunately, most of these are prescribed from without. The result is obviously more poverty.

It is important however, to note the emergence of globally competent African entrepreneurs and business leaders. These men and women have emerged from our ranks to become ambassadors of Africa in the highest levels of the world economy. Beside these 'world class' business leaders, there are many more in the various countries who are rising stars in every field imaginable.

While the colonial systems limited our potential, our own have liberated us to spread our wings and fly beyond what used to be the African's domain. Our institutes of training are producing relevantly trained and educated citizens. There is rising awareness for the need for continental partnership. As in the days of the struggle, African nations are beginning to concern themselves with what is happening beyond their boarders.

Seven

AFRICA'S CHALLENGES

The activity that characterised the turn of the century and the first decade of the new millennium signify a revival. It is plausible to believe that every single African must stand in his and her place to usher in this revival. All through history, major transitions have always come riding on the backs of strong and charismatic leaders. Africa like most of the world needs sound leadership. Not just powerful, but wise people as the previous eras had. We cannot stir the continent through these challenges with puny leadership.

This revival shall produce leaders and great people in all spheres of life. We are seeing a new breed of politicians, educators, business leaders, church leaders, farmers etc. It's a process of renewal, which everyone should participate in. Wherever you are and whatever you do, do it with all your might and with the best of your ability.

This generation of Africans will not go unnoticed. They shall make a mark from the international spheres down to the most remote village. African people are rising up and joining their hearts and hands as one man. We must count ourselves among them and in our hearts must burn the desire to see our people rise to their place of dignity and influence.

Awakening of the faith

It must be noted that Africa's rise is not her own but of God. It is the God of heaven who sets up times and seasons for nations and peoples of the world. Africa's revival is not due to some ancestral powers at play! It is entirely part of the season of God's grace.

All through history we see God in active play in the direction of the affairs of men. The rise of Africa's children is the fulfilment of many prophetic promises uttered over generations past and throughout scripture. We should be very careful not to ascribe to men and women abilities that are not due to them. God raised all the great sons and daughters of Africa and we must give to him all the glory and credit.

When Israel was in bondage in Egypt they cried out to God and he sent them a deliverer in the form of Moses. Alone the man was not any great leader (see Exodus 3). In fact, he had tried to defend an Israelite but had to flee for his life when the plan flopped. After 40 years he returned with the 'rod of God' in his hand and took Israel out with great exploits of God. Once in the Promised Land, Israel had a series of Judges and each one came as an answer to their cry to God and delivered them by the Spirit of God upon him. Whenever they would turn from their sins and serving other gods he would send them deliverance.

Many deceiving spirits have gone out throughout the world and Africa leading our people away from the one true God who created the earth and heaven. These teachings have manifested in the deification of men and women (dead or alive). The syncretic worship of ancestors, leaders, unknown spirits, and a host of other objects, natural and supernatural is gross error.

Western influences have given us science and atheism to doubt or deny the existence of God. However, this is changing. God is out to discredit the gods of our day and prove that He alone is to be worshiped throughout the length and breadth of the African continent.

As the apostle Paul said to the Corinthian church, God uses the 'foolish' things to shame the wise and the weak to shame the strong, so that none can boast before him. Africa's revival comes out of the power of God and the season and timing He set out for her.

Africa's Major Challenges

Africa like the rest of the world is facing serious challenges. In the forefront is the HIV/AIDS scourge. Second to it, are the wars that have been raging for years without end. Next come poverty and illiteracy. There are many more, but these are the most devastating of them all.

HIV and AIDS

The first public cases of HIV and AIDS in Africa were published in the early 1980s. As was the case in the rest of the world, there was very little knowledge about the virus and nobody took it seriously. But in just a few years it had grown to a pandemic. Millions perished and our generation was faced with potential decimation and was severely crippled on all fronts. Governments and society at large have been battling to control or manage the spread and devastation of the HIV and AIDS.

The impact on Africa has been enormous, as we have seen the millions of economically active people being wiped out daily. Nations have had to divert billions of dollars to research and acquisition of medicines for AIDS sufferers.

Awareness campaigns and wellness programs have taken a huge chunk of the budgets of these already poor countries. The frustration however is that as things stand, the infections still increase and death toll goes up. From just being a health issue, AIDS has become an all-encompassing issue for all Africa and the world at large.

Communities and families have been restructured to a point of dangerous imbalance. Single parent or no-parent households have become a common phenomenon. Orphans now constitute a significant portion of most African populations. These children bear the responsibility for their siblings too early in life that they lose their childhood in the process.

State welfare programs can't cope with the demand and refer the problems back to the society. It is a frightening vicious cycle. Gratefully, there are signs that the efforts are beginning to pay off. The tide is being stemmed albeit in a small way. The AIDS problem needs a lot of money and this is yet a problem in Africa.

2002 became a year of a string of legal battles in South Africa over the distribution and administration of the anti-retroviral drugs. Former South African president Thabo Mbeki is on record as claiming that AIDS is caused by poverty. He and the Health minister were called villains and many other nasty names. However, in Africa AIDS is really a multifaceted problem.

Beyond politics, religious leaders have also been drawn into the fray. Some are coping well while others are totally clueless. Unfortunately, there is as much diversity of opinion within the church as there is in the outside world. Obviously, the sexual abstinence argument is both religious and morally anchored. Many questions are raised on rights, ethics and individual freedom being infringed upon. It sometimes feels like the old chicken and egg story.

An HIV Free Generation

This does sound very naïve, even presumptuous in the face of current statistics. But this is the new direction that the fight against HIV/AIDS has taken in Africa. Several nations have posted positive results in their fight against the virus and the disease. Most are at least managing it effectively. Uganda, Botswana, Zimbabwe are some of the examples of nations that have attained significant positive results in their fight.

In Africa, the virus has been largely spread through heterosexual contact between an infected and an uninfected partner. The condom is generally viewed as a godsend for prevention.

All the pro-condom advocates, however, deliberately forget to tell that a condom, which if correctly used, still leaves the user with considerable vulnerability to contract the virus! If improperly used, the chances increase drastically. A condom is not as safe as it has been made to sound. Talking about safety, 'safe sex' is another overstressed preventive measure. This is supposed to refer to all sexual activity that reduces risk of exposure to the virus.

Essentially this approach says, be as promiscuous as you want, just prevent the contact of fluids with the virus. Amazingly, the pro 'safe sex' group is actively involved in the fight against HIV and are sometimes very aggressive against the abstinence group.

A moral society

Africa is a society of values and morals. Our communities have always hinged on clear definitions of right and wrong. There were no questions about whether something is acceptable or not. This approach governed the critical institutions of human relationships like family and marriage.

Ours, however, is a generation of low morals and cultural integration that disdains morality. The promotion sex without obligation is a sign of our downward slide. Sexuality is to be practised only in the parameters of the marriage relationship with one partner. This is important because once we begin to abuse it; we expose ourselves to dangerous consequences.

The issue of HIV/AIDS is essentially a moral. In the traditional African context, it was not permissible to abuse sex outside the parameters of the marriage relationship. Even in polygamous relationships, the same rule applied. Sadly, in many circles in the fight against HIV, there is increasing animosity against the 'moralist view.' However, success stories everywhere in the continent are attributed to positive morality.

Preserving the family institution

The African concept of family is expressed in community. One identifies with his close relatives as they do with their neighbour and the entire tribe and nation. The shared values are the code of conduct for all the members of the community. Defaulting is frowned upon and compliance is applauded corporately. The bond is weaker nowadays as people migrate, interface with other cultures and live further and longer apart. However, it is essential for the good morals to be promoted among our children. After all, the Bible gives us the same guidelines for family life.

A river between

Many an African community are now strangers one to the other because of the rivers that once brought them together. In the olden days, the communities that settled along the river were one. However, when the river became an international boundary, it tore these communities apart. We do ourselves disfavour if we do not acknowledge and promote the spirit of African brotherhood. If we view each other as foreign one to the other and even adopt xenophobic tendencies against each other, we are most to be pitied.

The year 2008 saw the most embarrassing incidents of tribal and national bigotry in Kenya and South Africa respectively. In 2004 South African were world heroes helping flood victims in Mozambique. Four years down the line they were butchering them in the name of xenophobia. Much can be said of other nations who did not make it to the headlines, yet perpetuate these shameful ways of hating their own brothers.

War and famine

Africa is a war-ravaged continent. Many parts of the motherland have not rested from war since the colonial era. As soon as the colonial masters were overthrown, the guns were turned on fellow countrymen. Untold savagery has been going on unabated. The consequences are obvious; displacement of people, massacres, famine and extensive suffering.

While there are many wars going on worldwide, most of Africa's wars are completely senseless. Many explanations have come as reasons for nations going off to war or people revolting against their governments. It is true that certain Western political powers use Africa as training ground for their weapons and make profits out of the fighting.

However, the blame lies on the African leadership. These warmongers in pursuit of their own selfish interests have dragged their nations to endless wars and defiantly resisted any attempts to negotiate for peace. These men and women enjoy the demise of the beautiful land. They are plunderers and terrorists of the worst kind. The pain and agony of the masses do not move their hearts. They have aborted many a nation's destiny and ruin that of Africa in the process.

They are proud and destructive. Nothing survives their sinister scheming. When they speak, they only deceive and have no regard to the treaties that they sign in total dishonesty. They are manipulative and their strength lies in their ability to divide the people for their personal gain and self-enrichment. Abuse of power and leadership authority is their speciality. If the individual ego of a leader is the reason why his forces are going to war or are still in the battlefield, then the cause is lost forever.

One only needs to look at the images of Angola's limbless and the Sudan and Somalia's starving millions. Sierra-Leone's weeping child-soldiers who were forced to kill their parents. We may also consider the million Rwandans who were victims of inspired tribal hate. If all these are not lessons for us, then our humane element is forever lost and we have degenerated to the level of animals.

Speaking out

I have seen a great tragedy in Africa. No one wants to take responsibility! Solving national problems takes more than just wishing for change. It requires full time meddling with the affairs! We have had the protests against globalisation, pollution etc., but fewer voices are heard when a nation is dragged into a senseless war or when a rebel movement seeks to topple a legitimate government. Wars spend lives and billions of precious cash and produce nothing but devastation in return.

In many African nations, the media has been left to fight a lone battle against tyranny and *'lootocracy'*. Where are the institutions that we set up with such pomp and pride, claiming they are set up to protect our people from tyranny?

Where are the people of Africa? Where is their conviction and conscience? Why do they only emerge as victims to claim compensation? If only we could be able to put our foot down for once and say, 'No to war and continuous bloodshed!' If only we could but speak up!

Bringing peace

Peace and reconciliation are not impossible ideals. After all every African flag or national anthem bears our aspiration for peace and prosperity! Why then is there no peace? Why are there fresh conflicts by day? It is because there is no serious commitment to pursuing peace.

There are a lot of attitudes and mind-sets that must be changed before the colours in our flags become the peace they symbolise. We must therefore make a serious commitment to build towards nationhood and corporate identity. We must uphold national ideals and respect the institutions.

Equity

In many African countries, there is a blatantly unfair treatment of minority groups. This has led to the consistent instability in our countries as people fight for their rights. Tribal segregation and inequitable appropriation of national resources is central to these feuds.

The government of national unity in many of our nations is a result of a forced compromise rather than a willing commitment to nationhood. As result it suffers from hidden selfish interest being smuggled into the pact, often with very damaging effects on trust.

This is not supporting 'rebellion with a cause'. It is equally unproductive to react violently to oppression. For a fact, fighting has never solved anything. There is no winner in any war. Those who take up arms lose more in the process than they hoped to achieve. It is better to win opinion than try to influence it by force!

When we deliberately pursue justice, we empower ourselves to succeed together and thus promote peace. The flipside is a rationalisation of injustice and other gross mistreatment of minorities. We should, however, seek more to foster a positive identity of brotherhood and seek to exploit our differences to advance our cause for nationhood.

In the same breath, this is a challenge to the tribalists, racists, and sowers of discord to desist from their divisive ways. Finally, it is a challenge to hold our leaders accountable for their actions and styles of governance. We must tolerate no longer the reasons they give for us to destroy one another without cause. We must see to it that perpetrators are brought to book.

Poverty and illiteracy

Africa is a rich continent, but its citizens are poor. There are many causes cited for poverty. However, the bulk of it can be traced to history and politics. In most African nations, the people are without means. Historically, the African ideal was for every household to own a piece of land to live on and produce their own food. With the advent of the new society these communities were shattered and their land rights lost.

Upon attainment of freedom, the new governments have failed to redress the issue of land and resources effectively. The Niger Delta, Zimbabwean farms and more recently the Libyan crisis are all representative of such failure. Vast majorities of African people live in their countries without means to afford a decent living.

All our major cities are known for their homeless, shack dwelling people. Because they have no basic education, they are without opportunity to learn and develop their potential to earn a better living. Living on under US$2 a day, they are forced to live without dignity. This norm is not normal!

Subtle Western influences

Many of our nations have come from behind to lead the world in a variety of disciplines. That is good and fair. However, there is a worrying factor in the development of the continent: the undue influence of the western sub-cultures and values. Surely with the world so shrunk, it is expected that cultures come into contact and people interact. The concern though is the use of one as an ideal for all.

Western cultures have been with us for more than a century. There has been a lot gained and yet also a lot lost. Afrocentrism and loyalty to the motherland has suffered greatly. Most of Africa's children have emigrated to the West never to return. In this day and age, however Africa needs people who cherish African values and these must represent her to the world better than the government's tourism department! The world's spotlight is on Africa but there seems to be so little coming from her.

One of the most worrying factors is that people who are experts on Africa are non-African! There are an amazing proportion of decisions about and for Africa made in the USA and Europe. Little wonder most are irrelevant and grossly inaccurate. Even our national politics is determined by the West. There is a very covert and, in some cases, not-so-subtle control of our continent by the western powers. The interference of the West in African issues is not tolerable, but often we feel we cannot do anything about it.

It takes one to look at who owns the most means of production in Africa to know that there is a new colonialism in place. We have seen African countries struggle with their foreign policy so that it complies with the expectations of western powers.

Call it democracy if you will, but it is unwarranted control of African affairs outsiders. Africa has never been accorded a fair partnership with her western counterparts. Instead our role has only been to co-operate and do as they say. We are bullied into compliance.

It is amazing how much we are buying into the fallacy that we cannot do anything by ourselves. One sees when we worship their heroes (and villains) and condemn our own people without second thought. Africa's failures and negatives are big news for western media. So much is the media propaganda that we begin to doubt the truth we know. So much has the music and movies from Hollywood have we consumed that ours sound dull and incomplete. What we fail to realise though is that we have such a rich heritage and plenty room to improve.

Is Africa better than the West? No. Nor is the opposite true. Rather each can be better *with* the other. It is necessary at this stage to complement rather than compare. There is mutual benefit in equal interaction. As long as the Africans view the West as their Canaan, then they will not see the greatness in themselves.

Part 4

THE FUTURE OF THE MOTHERLAND

Eight

WHERE ARE WE HEADED?

It is important after examining the past and present of Africa to take a good look at the future. The past is fixed and cannot be changed. There is an expression that goes; 'What is done is done'. We can only draw lessons from it and inspiration to influence our current and future behaviour. We have an opportunity though to contribute to our future in a very meaningful way.

Firstly, it is important for us to assume responsibility for how things will go from here onwards. Once we have done that, then we must put in place strategies for transformation. Finally, we must work hard and constantly evaluate our success.

Vision

Where there is no vision the people cast off restraint. (Prov 18).

Vision is the ability to sustain a focused and purposeful cause with specific tasks and responsibilities constantly engaged. Vision is essential for nations as well as individuals. If it is lacking, people tend to wander in life unprofitably experiencing one day after the other. There is no direction or measurable progress.

Africa's future needs visionaries. People who can see something and can help others see it too. NEPAD was supposed to be vision of Africa developed by Africans. Sadly, it seems to have died a quiet death. Many African states embraced the illusion that political freedom was all there was to freedom.

Few of our countries have a defined national vision. In many emerging African democracies, the future is defined in terms of the struggle, i.e. in retrospect. However, a political vision must give Africa a sense of purpose and something to look for in the future. A vision is not reality. It is a plan for the future. It is in the pursuit and implementation that we are found wanting.

The prophet Habakkuk penned one of scripture's most profound statements:

> And the Lord answered and said, write the vision and make it plain upon tables that he may run that readeth it. For the vision is for an appointed time, but at the end it shall speak, and not lie, though it tarry wait for it because it shall surely come. It will not tarry. (Habakkuk 2v2-3)

Vision must be clear, communicated and its fulfilment patiently pursued. Many visions have been put forth, but they were unclear and illegible. Others were long in coming and abandoned. However, Africa's future needs clear vision and a hopeful people to catch the same. Africa needs a new vision in every sphere. It is impossible to lift a continent without one all-embracing vision. I pray God would raise us a generation and those who will read the vision of a new Africa and run with it.

Education

Knowledge is power indeed. A basic definition of education is the impartation of knowledge and skills to effect a permanent life transformation. Africa's way forward is for her masses to be educated. Reading unlocks many doors and writing breaks barriers to the flow of knowledge. It is vital that much be invested in Africa's education system and institutions. An illiterate people are always automatically excluded from information and their contribution does not count.

An educated society is empowered to be tolerant of diversity and comfortable with differences that may be found within it. The new global trends demand that Africa step forward and deliver. As pointed out earlier, Africa has several outstanding representatives to the world, but they are not adequate in proportion of the vast continental potential. Our constant effort must be directed at developing this potential at grassroots level and thus raise the whole of society together.

A few flying arrows with no back up will accomplish very little. We must desist from consoling ourselves that we have a representative. Africa must prepare her children to face the real challenges of the future. For too long we have had an African representation at international levels that have no knowledge of the situation on the ground.

This representation is divorced from the real concerns of the African people. It is unrealistic to expect non-African organisations to save Africa. We must rise up and put our future on our agenda and work as best as we can. It is time that the AU, our respective governments and African NGOs and businesses invested in the education of our people in totality. Giving our people education is giving then a key to any door of their choice in the future. It is giving them a privilege that none can take from them, a heritage of unparalleled value.

We cannot expect to be saved by the donations from abroad. We are to be regarded as legitimate team members whose cause others can support. We must take the full responsibility for our people and our future. As Africans, we must invest in the education of our people so as to secure a better future enabling them to be in a position to better their lives.

The love of our people

For centuries Americans have taken a solemn pledge of patriotism from their childhood throughout their lives. This way their pride is fostered and their love for fellow Americans is nurtured throughout. In the face of the fateful September 11, the nation demonstrated this bond as they sought help from God and in one another. There comes a time when your love for your own people is tested. When that day comes, your love better not be sentimental!

The African Diaspora

One of our greatest limitations has been that we have 'another place to go to.' Don't we see Africans run away from their lands and problems to Europe and America? It is not emigration that is a problem, but if we always keep escape alternatives open, we will never learn to be independent.

When other lands suffered their own depressions and trials they stayed and fought. Their efforts and not donations saved their lands! One thinks of the millions of Africans in Diaspora.

How she longs for their return to rebuild her broken societies and repair her devastation. The promise of the scattered Israel through the prophet is striking in its hopeful tone;

> Your people will rebuild the ancient ruins and will raise up the age-old foundations; you will be called Repairer of the Broken Walls, Restorer of Streets with Dwellings. (Isaiah 58v12)

It was the returning volunteers that raised the walls of the Temple and the city in Jerusalem. It is the people who must take responsibility for their own nation.

Today there are millions of Africans scattered in all the nations of the world. They got there because of different circumstances. Some left as refugees because of war, others to seek better opportunities, but what remains is that they are 'sons and daughters of the soil.' These often have an obvious added value in the form of education, financial opportunity and fruitful links.

It is at times like these that we look to them for a contribution towards the rebuilding of the continent. It is such individuals that we count on to represent the true African values and the millions of us who share the African spirit. It is these that we expect to invest in the future of the communities that raised them.

The African Child

Without doubt, the future of the continent is predicated in its posterity. The seed of a people is important for the perpetuation of their species. The purpose and destiny of a people depends on the future generations. Hence the children play a very important role in the survival of the generations to come. The future depends on the present. It is with this realisation that we must focus our resources on the development of the African child. In the olden days, the child was an important part of society and children were raised in such a way they started participating in the life of their society at a very early stage.

The modern era brought with it education and basic rights and protection for the children that give them a better outlook to life. The challenge that we face is to ensure that these are provided for every African child. A home, education, healthcare, safety and indeed a childhood are the basic rights that every African child must get to keep the future of the continent insured.

Today, a growing number of our children are homeless and live in the streets of our cities. The problem has refused to go away despite our throwing pennies at it. We must do something about the so-called 'street children', 'child-headed families' and 'child soldiers.' All these terms are a reverse of normalcy. Few children if any are on the street because they are just delinquent.

Many are there because of a compound of problems at home. They run away from abuse and violence directed at them in the homes where they ought to be safe. For some, there is just no more home as they have lost parents to the HIV/AIDS scourge.

The UN declaration of children's rights has been evaluated with derision, as it is perceived as a westernised approach to child bringing whose values are on the extreme. Yet if examined more closely, we will see that it is not different to the African aspirations to raising children.

In Africa, a child is the future and that makes our children an endangered species. It is in Africa that the sayings; 'Everyone's child' and 'It takes a village to raise a child' originated. The collective responsibility of ensuring that our children are raised in the ways of our people, proud to be African, is ours.

The African Youth

The old era valued youths and welcomed them into adulthood in the most elaborate ways. Our political freedom was won through the direct involvement of many youths. Who can forget the protesting Soweto schoolchildren in 1976, the *mujibhas* of the Zimbabwean liberation war? Yet in many an African country they are seen as a bother rather than an asset and next in line in the advancement of the cause of Africa.

African youth are among the continent's most crucial resources. Young people are as vital to Africa as they are to any society because they are strong and goal oriented. The future and direction that this continent shall take will be determined by the calibre of young people that we shall produce. It is of great importance that we begin to nurture an African oriented youth all over this continent. This is a youth that sees possibilities and potential in our land and shall not succumb to pessimistic opinions that are peddled by the rest of the world.

One of the serious concerns about today's young people is their apathy. There has been a break in commitment from the pre-independence Africa to the present generation. The trend to aspire to a 'hippie' lifestyle is a serious threat to the continent's future.

We have raised a materialistic generation that was babysat by MTV. Very few of our young people are interested in the affairs; let alone the future of their nations. Yet there are grave issues to be tackled, issues that will determine our survival as a people.

The tendency to manipulate the young people to achieve selfish political ends is rife in Africa. Many have been politicised to commit atrocities against their own people and in the process filled with hate and violence. No one seems to want to let the young people contribute to life except nominally.

We have seen frustrated potential as those who are older refuse to create space or step down to let the younger generation carry on the noble task of nation building.

The apprehension about the young spoiling the vision has only bred apathy and disillusionment in Africa. Young people no longer aspire to great positions, as they know that such is a waste of time. Instead they have settled to a mediocre but more certain position of just-get-a-job-survive approach. Unfortunately, this will not get us far in this quest for advancement.

We are currently lamenting the massive brain drain, where the finest of our professionals have left to serve other people. Why should we, if we are not prepared to remunerate them effectively? And so, our youth leave for 'green pastures' where they will be under-utilised but paid enough to survive, a compromise that many have gladly embraced.

We must invest in our youth the vision of our national aspirations and the future that we desire for Africa. The condescending attitude of many political, religious and even corporate institutions towards young people is disturbing. They always seem to view the young people as immature and inadequate. Their contributions and needs are seen as secondary and unimportant.

This must change. The younger generation is a very important component in this race as they are receiving the button and will determine the outcome of the race. Sure, enough the young need the old for guidance and moderation but the old also need the young to keep the race alive. If this approach is implemented, we should expect more progress and less resistance to the unfolding of the new era of Africa.

Nine

AS A NATION THINKS

The African Student Movement

One of Africa's most effective change agents is the student movement. The African University campuses have for long served as the breeding ground for change. The African Liberation movement was born here and to date significant ideological influences come from the campuses. Needless to say, there is still a great potential. There are significant challenges however, with regard to harnessing this potential today.

Firstly, many African countries have left these institutions to decay and become run down without any capacity to influence the greater society. The very standards of education have sunk so low the society has no more regard for the social authority that the institutions used to be.

Most of Africa's great once universities have long become institutions to stifle actual thinking. Some political and other ideological groupings have continued to exploit the student population to a significant extent. Although for some it has been manipulation, for others it was a legitimate tapping of the youth potential.

Nearly every significant national awakening comes riding on the back of the student movement. Most of these self-appointed society watchdogs led the campaign against the corrupt government officials and in some cases resulting in removal of corrupt regimes. These students went on to be legislators and politicians of note. The activism they initiated saw in several countries, a change of heart toward the educational policies.

Mere Academics

Education's aim is to produce a well-formed person. At least that was at the heart of the foundation of the learning institution. The institution of learning was designed to result in the change a person's behaviour so as to add value to the society.

Today though, we see the institution churning our certificate-wielding people who have a parasitic effect on society. The so-called educated citizens are merely academics who know facts and not truth! Universities today have become hollow caves that have little to do with society's development. We have come to the age where "education does not educate."

Initiating Change

Over the years, two ingredients have always been essential among the youth these are power and knowledge. A generation that is not knowledgeable has always been a weak one. All nations spend millions on educating their youth. There is one variable though, that will affect the effectiveness of this expenditure i.e. what they learn. There are those who gain destructive power and use it. There are those who gain constructive and problem-solving power and put it to use.

While a new African student regime is emerging out of a host disadvantages, there is one very worrying factor. They have not yet learnt the confidence to be proactive and take a risk, for themselves and the rest of their people. African youths largely were raised in an environment of *aspiration and not inspiration.*

The boundaries were already set and the best would be judged by how near they got close to the ceiling. Of course, there were some significant numbers who went beyond these fantastic heroes! In many African counties, we still operate organisations founded in 1900! We just keep rotating the leadership. Not fresh ideas.

No one has bothered to look at the situation's manifold transition over the years. Most of these organisations are oversubscribed and perform far below basic acceptable standards. These become sacred cows that we only pride ourselves in by name and not with our heart.

The age of Entrepreneurship

Sometimes it is amazing the poor of the earth are believed to deserve. If you followed the activities of many relief organisations (almost all western), you can be amazed by the 'innovative' methods that have been taught the poor to survive. In India, they might be funded to collect cow dung 'fuel'.

In Africa, they might be on some bone collecting projects. While these projects may be generating income, they reduce dignity and stifle the mind and pacify the drive to be creative.

We are almost always bundled together in group thinking and predetermined activities.

Entrepreneurship Defined

Entrepreneurship is the process of value and opportunity creation as well as excelling in business and development of wealth creating ideas. No one has the monopoly of this. Its goal is to generate and multiply. Its aims to have a ripple effect on the economy. The creation and management of resources and wealth is implied. A vast majority of us are familiar with the creation (as workers) and have little access to the control side of wealth.

We want to believe that the African has come to the age of empowerment and equality. That is not so however, as long as Africans are still the majority customer base in trade and commerce.

Nice sounding terms like SMME have forever given us the aspiration and pride of street corner shop ownership or a trouser patching home run business. There is need for Africa to develop her capacity for being productive in a creative way. It is imperative that we revisit the kind of education offered in the school, the facilities available at community level and the exposure to the outside world. These factors have a significant bearing in the ignition of inspiration.

The businesspeople of yesteryear copied their white counterparts, and none left a legacy for future generations. They were players in the uneven field and restricted by legislation and other structures that were designed against them. The new generation of entrepreneurs though, must rise up to seize the opportunities. It is the spirit of entrepreneurship that has ushered in the famed economic revivals in the world.

The Professionals of Africa

We are in need for those people who will do whatever they have to do well enough that it will make a difference. One of Africa's resource siphons are professionals that do not deliver. These people have a training that often cost the state or their family lots of money, but they deliver far too less than what they are expected to do. It is a legitimate expectation that professions can be used to shape a society that we desire to build. Unfortunately, we are now in the stage where all that matters is how much we are paid rather than what we produce. We long for people who will use their professional training to contribute to Africa's quest for revival.

Skilled personnel changed the face of Europe and Asia. They were the brains and hands behind the industrial as well as the electronic revolutions. Skills development is not the preserve of Government. Ancient Africa was a skills development and transfer world. The elders apprenticed the youths and those who are willing to acquire the skill. Today we have a compartmentalised society where skills development is left for the specialised institutions. An average adult has no special skills except what they do in their job (if they are even skilled at all).

Africa's biggest challenge is the great brain drain. The massive exportation of skills and the underutilised potential continue to plague many African countries. Sadly, very little effort is paid to develop skills at continental level. Continental bodies like the AU tend to prioritise political and trade issues rather than research and skills development. The initiative is left to the private sector that unfortunately do not have the network and universal mandate that the continental and regional bodies have.

The Senior Citizens of Africa

An alarming phenomenon has crept up in Africa, where we like our western counterparts are isolating the few remaining senior citizens to old people's homes. There is no hopeless society than that which has no wisdom of the grey haired amongst them.

The younger generation tends to seek convenience, but the older folks bring the much-needed balance in our lives. This applies both for a small community as well as the leadership of a nation. Who does not envy South Africa for having Mandela? We as a continent need to have the covering of respectable b*azees* over the affairs of our land.

The value of age

It is amazing that every generation looks to the previous for standards and values. Society seems to progress further and further from what is seen as upright and esteemed. Biblical evidence shows us that the older people are highly esteemed. The Bible and African society places great value on the older folks.

They were never assigned to Old aged homes or abandoned as we now see. Take for instance the blessings of God being passed on by the aged patriarch. Abraham instructs his children in the ways of the Lord from a hundred years old! Isaac requests his favourite dish to release the blessing on his firstborn when his eyes no longer see anything. Jacob blesses his and Joseph's sons on his deathbed. When Joseph is dying, he gives the instruction to take his bones out of Egypt and they did. David is on his deathbed when he confers the kingdom over Solomon.

The elders have a great role to play in building the fibre and future of our continent. Sadly, most of them are hidden in the rural areas and old people's homes where they are 'cared for' so that they may not interfere with our progress. Our elders have a contribution to the future of our people. It is wise for the younger to consult them while they live rather than attempt to do so when they are dead!

Ten

BRINGING CHANGE

There are a thousand and one prescriptions that can help to tackle the odds that face us as a people. It should be noted that there are many thousands of concerned and actively engaged Africans working to reverse the curse. We shall here put forth yet another proposition that is simple enough to be used by all of us. Not all of will be able to sit in the houses of power to deliberate the future of the motherland. But in a small way we can all put in something substantial that will be much at the end.

The GAP principle seeks to involve everyone everywhere to participate in the building of the continent. It focuses primarily on the young and upcoming Africans. One of today's tragedies as already discussed, is the *passivity* of the youth. The future of families, nations and continent is in great risk because of this attitude.

It is true that if the plight of Africa is not 'my responsibility' now before we have the resources, power and authority to bring about significant changes, then we will not do so when we get them. Africa's leading crises include among others; HIV/AIDS, poverty, ethnic conflicts, famines, family disintegration and unemployment. Do these things mean anything to our youth? What are their personal opinions on each one of these? Are they keeping up with the trends in society? Are our youth only victims and respond by complaining and blaming someone for it?

> And again I looked and saw the oppression that was taking place under the sun: I saw the tears of the oppressed - and they have no comforter; Power was on the side of their oppressors - and they have no comforter...

It is important for us to help them to *feel* something if they will be able to respond to these issues in a way that will help bring about change. If we do not *learn* to be moved by situations that we see now, we will never do so when we have the power to *do* something about them.

Our generation is so focussed only on itself and not God, or on the plight of others (Luke 18v2-4). We must be able to *visualise* real people with real needs. Angola should mean 27 years of devastation and thousands of refugees and limbless victims of landmines. It is often people from outside Africa that end up doing something. What does the plight of Africa mean to you personally? Overexposure in the media has led to insensitivity. We tend to see the plight of others as just 'stories' and brush them aside.

Nehemiah 1v4 reveals a different attitude to the news that Jerusalem is in ruin. He demonstrates deep concern for his nation. He takes it personally and weeps and fasts for several days and immediately undertakes to *do something* about it. His response was; 'This is not the way things should be'.

He refused to accept the ruined state of Jerusalem as normal. Neither did he blame the Babylonians who did it. Some of us accept the ruined state of Africa as normal or unchangeable. We must not! We *can* change it and we *must* change it.

God is already concerned. We must align ourselves with his concern for Africa and make ourselves available to.

> Your people will rebuild ancient ruins and will raise up age-old foundations; you will be called Repairer of Broken Walls, Restorer of Streets with Dwellings. (Isaiah 58v12)
>
> They will rebuild ancient ruins and repair places long devastated; they will renew the ruined cities that have been devastated for generations. (Isaiah 61v4)

G is for Giving

> Out of ...their extreme poverty welled up in rich generosity... they gave as much as they were able, and even beyond their ability. Entirely on their own, they pleaded with us for the privilege of sharing... (2 Cor 8v2-4)

It takes money, time, materials and support to meet a need. For a long time, Africa has always looked outwards for help. While it is true that we should expect external help, we must learn to give to worthwhile causes among us. It is true that there are enough resources to meet and surpass our needs but we have not learned to expend ourselves on behalf of others.

This spirit of generosity is fast disappearing in Africa. We seem to be addicted to hand-outs and 'free packages'! This is not only irresponsibility but also a shameful way of conducting ourselves and certainly inhibiting our blessing. As the Scripture says: 'It is more blessed to give than to receive.'

In our society today, those who have the resources spend them recklessly in hyper luxurious lifestyles. Bono, the Irish rock musician of U2 began an international campaign to address the plight of Africa. He not only lobbied for the cancellation of the debt of the continent, but also put in millions of his own money. This he said was a gesture of appreciation for the life that the people who supported his music career had afforded him. What a challenge to those who are privileged to have!

I have seen some of our own people invest in personal luxury what could have benefited thousands of their fellow people in terms of basic needs. We must teach ourselves once again the African values of giving and communal existence. Donate to a worthy cause. Raise funds for a project to improve the lives of other people. It is ridiculous that Americans would be more involved in helping our own people to get water to drink and basic sanitation. We must not wait for some foreign NGO to start a charity to meet the needs of our people.

A is for Advocacy

> Speak out for those who cannot speak for themselves, for the rights of the destitute, speak up and judge fairly, defend the rights of the poor and the needy. (Prov 31v8-9)

In Africa, it seems nobody wants to make another's business theirs. We live in an age of expression and must speak out and raise opinion. It is evident that good things don't just happen they must be spoken for. Neither do people toe the line on their own. They must be confronted. Someone must speak up.

There is a lure to the indifferent side of the street and we are in need for a constant reminder. Too many people are waiting for someone to stir them up and then they will get up and do something. There is too little conviction in our generation and we need people to stir us up to action.

If all you can give is your voice, then add it on! Write something down and it will never be forgotten nor easily ignored. Many have done a great deal in contributing to society by talking about issues. Become an activist, a blogger, fight for a cause, and raise awareness. The pen is always mightier than the sword.

The victory against Apartheid in South Africa may be partly attributed to song. The musicians rose up and composed hopeful tunes that sustained the struggle even in the face of bitter oppression. The same is claimed for the African American slaves. Martin Luther King's *I have a Dream*, sermon lives to this day. Others sang their way to freedom. It is good to sing if only to inspire someone towards a corporate goal. The 'Arab Spring' of 2011 was reform by protest. People stood up and spoke in one voice. They said, 'Enough is enough!'

Tools of Democracy

The ballot is the most powerful tool in democracy. It is the exercise of one's right to choose or reject. However, many people in the Motherland have long abandoned faith in the ballot box. True, there has been lots of rigging, but that does not warrant our abandonment of this vital tool of expression. Go and vote when you have to. 'Your vote' as they always say, 'is your voice'.

The new millennium saw a rise in the number of demonstrations against such things as globalisation, war and economic oppression. This is an outward show of one's opposition to something they believe is wrong and a great way to inspire opinion. It is important for us to join the march and carry the banners.

We must publicly condemn those things that are destructive to our societies. In certain parts of Africa this is usually with a price but it is worth the while. It is powerful to verbalise our conviction.

P is for Prayer

> I urge you, then, first of all that requests, prayers, intercession and thanksgiving be made for everyone-for kings and all those in authority that we may live a peaceful and quiet lives in all godliness and holiness. This is good and pleases God our Saviour who wants all men to be saved and to come to the knowledge of the truth. (1Tim 2v1-4)

All transformation has its roots in prayer. Someone once wrote so accurately:

> "Men may spurn our appeals, reject our message, oppose our arguments, despise our persons; but they are helpless against our prayers."

It is important for the believers to pray for the wellbeing of their nations and indeed for those who have the responsibility to make decisions that affect our day to day lives. The Bible and the history of the Christian faith bear witness to the prevailing prayers of the saints.

The Bible does not encourage us in vain to pray for our nations and those in positions of authority. Note that Paul encourages the believers to pray so that we may lead a holy and peaceable life. We must pray for situations as you meet them and also encourage others to pray.

The habit of turning the newspaper page or flipping to another more TV interesting channel must cease. We must mature to the stage where the reported plight of other people becomes our prayer burden. When will God raise us up in the middle of the night with a vision of the 'man from Macedonia?' When will we take in our prayer schedules the countries and people whose names we cannot even pronounce well, simply because God's spirit lays a burden on us to do so?

Prayer is not to be confined to the church alone but the entire nation must be brought to God, especially those who are leaders. As we saw in the previous chapter, the spiritual connection of a nation will determine its prosperity. The Bible gives us several glimpses of national prayer and God undertaking for them.

> If my people who are called by name shall humble themselves, and seek my face and turn away from their wickedness, then will I hear them from heaven and heal their land. (2 Chronicles 7v14)

Prayer however is not only for occasional purposes either, but a vocation for life. Africa now needs praying people. The continent is at a time when 'the children have come to birth but there is no strength to deliver.' Will you commit yourself to take a stand for the sake of Africa today? Do you see yourself playing a part in making Africa's problems your prayer responsibility?

God is in Africa

After all, has been said and done, one wants to ask the crucial question: Where does God fit in African picture? This is an essential question because without him, there is not hope or future to talk about. Africa is in dire need for God's intervention. It is a continent whose repentance must precede revival. Africa may be viewed in pity, yet she also needs the prophet's goading words to motivate her to repentance. History tells stories of God's workings with the peoples of the nations of the world. He is consistent in all his dealings with the nations and calls them to account.

Contrary to the idea of Africa seeking God, He has been waiting for the great continent to respond to His love. *"Ethiopia (Africa) shall soon stretch her hands to God"* God's invitation for Africa has been standing for ages. Generation after generation has ignored his call. As Israel of old, the prospect of Western sophistication has been our preoccupation and pursuit. The emergence of the New World views and secular philosophies has been alluring. We are increasingly expecting emancipation by those who put us in bondage in the first place. Yet God's voice reminds us to **"remember the rock from where we were hewn..."** That rock is our salvation.

Postscript

WHAT SHALL WE DO THEN ABOUT THIS?

One of today's tragedies is that of insensitivity. Overexposure to a host of evils breeds indifference. The issues that are discussed in this book are not unfamiliar. In fact, this book sought to present the general opinion of the ordinary citizen of Africa. There may be some of us who hold a different opinion in some or all the contents of this book. That is not a problem. It is good for opinion to vary. However, it is important for us to now answer the most important question of all: What shall you do about these issues?

The Africa we live in is increasingly sophisticated with evil masquerading as culture. We must fight to awaken the conscience. We must strive to preserve the dignity of the African peoples from commercialisation, where we are tourist souvenirs. We must speak for ourselves and not rely on others to fight for us as if we were some endangered species! We must ensure justice and equity prevails in our societies in authentic community leadership.

We must demonstrate initiative and be innovative rather than wait helplessly for someone to save us. Above all we must turn one and all to God. Africa is an original continent. We did not migrate from elsewhere to settle in this land. It is our heritage and we must tap into the God given capacity. We must look up to the God of heaven from whom all humanity derives its purpose and then forward to the future.

SEASONS OF AFRICA

www.ingramcontent.com/pod-product-compliance
Lightning Source LLC
Chambersburg PA
CBHW020947090426
42736CB00010B/1297